Prehistoric North America

When Life Took Root on Land

The Late Paleozoic Era

Jean F. Blashfield with Richard P. Jacobs

© 2006 Heinemann Library
a division of Reed Elsevier Inc.
Chicago, Illinois

Customer Service 888-454-2279
Visit our website at www.heinemannlibrary.com

Produced for Heinemann Library by Books Two, Inc.
Editorial: Jean Black, Deborah Grahame
Design: Michelle Lisseter
Illustrations: John T. Wallace, Top-Notch Productions
Picture Research: JLM Visuals
Production: Jean Black

Originated by Modern Age Repro
Printed and bound by South China Printing Company

10 09 08 07 06
10 9 8 7 6 5 4 3 2 1

Library of Congress Cataloging-in-Publication Data
Blashfield, Jean F.
  When life took root on land / Jean F. Blashfield and Richard P. Jacobs.
    p. cm. -- (Prehistoric North America)
  Includes bibliographical references and index.
  ISBN 1-4034-7659-4
  1. Fossils--Juvenile literature. 2. Paleontology--Juvenile literature. 3.
Geology, Stratigraphic--Paleozoic. I. Jacobs, Richard P. II. Title. III.
Series: Blashfield, Jean F. Prehistoric North America.
  QE714.5.B5 2005
  560'.175--dc22   2004027489

560.175
BLA
c. 1

Geology Consultant: Marli Bryant Miller, Ph.D., University of Oregon
Maps: Ronald C. Blakey, Ph.D., Northern Arizona University
PHOTO CREDITS: COVER: Reptile fossil, Richard P. Jacobs; Crossbedded sandstone in Northern Arizona, Breck P. Kent.
TITLE PAGE: Balanced rock at Mexican Hat, Utah, Richard P. Jacobs
INTERIOR: Amundson, Burton A.: 51; Balkwell, David: 72 Archean; Blegen, Don: 43 top left; Brockus, Lloyd R.: 43 bot left;
Cokendolpher, J.C.: 42; Crangle, Charlie: 73 Jurassic; Cress, Alan: 36 top left; The Field Museum: 6, 8 top, 28, 37 left, 38 left, 40 left,
44 bot, 46, 47, 48, 72 Cambrian, Silurian, Permian, 73 Paleocene, Miocene, Pliocene; Gilbert, Gordon R.: 73 Eocene; Greenler,
Robert: 12; Harms, Carl: 54; Jacobs, Richard P.: 5, 8 bot, 9 bot, 14, 20, 22 top, 22 bot, 27, 31 top, 32 top, 33 top, 33 bot, 34 top,
34 bot, 35 bot left, 35 bot right, 36 bot, 37 right, 38 right, 40 right, 41 top, 43 top right, 49, 50 second down, 50 third down, 50 bot,
56 top, 56 bot, 58, 61 right, 69 bot; Kent, Breck P.: 16 top, 30 bot, 32 center, 32 bot, 36 top right, 39 bot, 41 bot, 43 bot right,
45 top, 45 center, 45 bot, 53, 60, 61 left, 67 top, 71, 72 Ordovician, Devonian, Mississippian, 73 Holocene; Kerstitch, Alex: 31 bot;
Laudon, Lowell R.: 9 top, 19, 50 top, 51 bot; Leszczynski, Zig: 73 Oligocene; Miller, Marli: 4, 52, 57 bot, 64, 70, 73 Pleistocene;
Minnich, John: 30 top, 65; NASA: Page borders, 23; NASA/Artist Don Davis: 67 bot; NPS: 21; Reblin, Mike: 16 bot; Smithsonian
National Museum of Natural History: 26, 39 top, 55, 72 Proterozoic, Pennsylvanian; USGS: 66, 68, 69 top; University of Kansas
Natural History Museum: 39 top inset, 41 center, 44 top; University of Michigan Exhibit Museum: 35 top, 62, 73 Triassic.

Some words are shown in bold, **like this**. You can find the definitions for these words in the glossary.

Contents

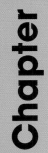

The Scene as the Late Paleozoic Started

Chapter 1

Our lives today depend a great deal on what happened on Earth more than 300 million years ago. Plants living then eventually turned into **coal**. We burn coal to make electric power. The swamp plants that became coal are the best example of what happened, as the title of this book says, "when life took root on land."

More than half the time known as the late Paleozoic was the amazing period when living things spread everywhere possible. They also began to reach huge sizes. Giant trees, monstrous salamanders, and dragonflies the size of crows appeared during this time.

This book might also be called "when life almost died." The latter half of the Paleozoic Era ended in a dramatic **mass extinction**. Events came terribly close to wiping out all the living things that had developed in the first half of the Paleozoic.

Geologists are scientists who first described geologic time—the many millions of years during which Earth developed as we know it today. They were most concerned with life and the **fossils** left behind in rock. They call the entire time for which there is a rock record of fossil shells Phanerozoic time. *Phanerozoic* in Greek means "revealed life."

The Phanerozoic is broken into three main time segments. They are the Paleozoic Era, meaning "ancient life;" the Mesozoic Era, or "middle life;" and the Cenozoic Era, or "recent life." We are still in the Cenozoic today.

↰ *The fossil of a dragonfly from the late Paleozoic*

↰ *The swamps of the Florida Everglades are thought to resemble the swamps that fed the coal-making process during the late Paleozoic.*

The Paleozoic Era

The first part of the Paleozoic is called the Cambrian Period. Everything before that—about 88 percent of our planet's story—is known as *Pre*cambrian. The complete **geologic time scale** can be found on pages 72 and 73.

The Paleozoic began about 543 million years ago. Geologists designated the start of the Paleozoic to correspond with a seemingly sudden appearance of abundant fossils. These fossils were those of shelled animals from ancient shallow seas that had covered the land. Actually, there had already been 3 billion years of living things. Their soft bodies left few traces behind, however. Then animals acquired shells. As a result, many more identifiable fossils became part of rock. Fossil-making animals flourished in the seas that covered much of the land. They **evolved** and changed, preparing to take over the land.

The first part of the Paleozoic Era consists of four periods. During these periods, almost all groups of living things got their start. These periods are the Cambrian, Ordovician, Silurian, and Devonian. The Devonian set the scene for the second part of the Paleozoic, which started with the Carboniferous Period.

The later part of the Paleozoic is broken up into only two periods. The first of these is the Carboniferous. It is the longest period of Phanerozoic time.

↰ *This model of a Devonian **cephalopod** was based on fossil discoveries. Such octopus ancestors were common during the late Paleozoic Era.*

PALEOZOIC ERA • *543 to 248 million year ago*

	Time Period	Tectonic Events	Biological Events
PHANEROZOIC TIME • *543 million years ago to present* · PALEOZOIC ERA • *543 to 248 million years ago*	**Cambrian Period** *543–248 million years ago* Named for old name of Wales	Laurentia separated from Siberia	Cambrian Explosion: Major diversification of marine invertebrates
	Ordovician Period *490–443 million years ago* Named for a Celtic tribe in Wales	First Iapetus Ocean Taconic orogeny in northeastern Laurentia	First true vertebrates: jawless fish First land plants Mass extinction
	Silurian Period *443–417 million years ago* Named for a Celtic tribe in Wales	Caledonian orogeny Shallow seas on Laurentia	First vascular plants First insects First jawed fish
	Devonian Period *417–354 million years ago* Named for Devon, England	Major reef building	First forests First seed–baring plants First four–footed animals First amphibians
CARBONIFEROUS PERIOD *354 to 290 million years ago*	**Mississippian Epoch** *354–323 million years ago* Named for Mississippi River Valley	Antler orogeny	Ferns abundant First land vertebrates
	Pennsylvanian Epoch *323–290 million years ago* Named for coal formations in Pennsylvania	Appalachian orogeny began	Ferns abundant Major coal–forming forests First reptiles
	Permian *290–248 million years ago* Named for Russian province of Perm	Pangea formed	First warm–blooded reptiles Greatest mass extinction

MESOZOIC ERA • *248 to 65 million years ago*
CENOZOIC ERA • *65 million years ago to present*

The Carboniferous is named for the huge quantities of the material that became coal—primarily the chemical element carbon—deposited during this time. Plants that grew during the Carboniferous eventually died, rotted, were buried, and became coal. The second, or last, period in the Paleozoic is called the Permian Period. It is named after rocks found near Perm in Russia. The series of death-dealing events at the end of the Paleozoic is called the **Permian Extinction** (see Chapter 5).

The Carboniferous

Everywhere in the world except North America, the Carboniferous Period is one long span of time. It lasted from 354 million years ago to about 290 million years ago. However, different events were taking place in North America—on the ancient continent called **Laurentia**—than happened elsewhere. Because of this difference, North Americans generally break the Carboniferous into two shorter times called **epochs**. It includes the Mississippian Epoch and the Pennsylvanian Epoch.

The Mississippian Epoch in North America goes from 354 to 323 million years ago. The primary rocks associated with this time are from the Mississippi River Valley. They are fossil-bearing **limestone**. These were formed in the **marine** environment of the shallow sea that covered most of Laurentia. Limestone is the mineral calcium carbonate. Certain kinds of **algae** (seaweeds) consist largely of this mineral. When the algae die, the mineral solids fall to the seafloor. Also, the shells of many marine animals that were abundant in the ancient sea consist of calcium carbonate.

Particularly common among the animals were **crinoids**. These are related to today's starfish. Crinoids grew abundantly in the shallow sea. As a result, the areas where their fossils are found are often called crinoid meadows. The Mississippi River Valley in the central United States has crinoid limestone deposits that may be more than 500 feet (150 m) thick.

The second part of North America's Carboniferous is called the Pennsylvanian Epoch. It lasted from 323 to 290 million years ago. More plants that turn into the rocks called coal were deposited than at any other time in Earth history. We'll learn more about Pennsylvanian coal in Chapter 4.

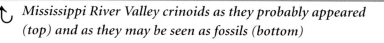

Mississippi River Valley crinoids as they probably appeared (top) and as they may be seen as fossils (bottom)

The Limestone Landscape of Western Kentucky

Much limestone and its resulting landforms can be seen in western Kentucky. The limestone layer was formed during the Mississippian. It is responsible for the unusual landforms seen in the area.

Limestone easily dissolves in water. As a result, vast areas of rock located here dissolved away. Numerous caves are found in western Kentucky. The world's largest known cave, Mammoth Cave, is one of these. The Mammoth Cave system has so far been mapped to be at least 360 miles (580 km) long. It may be even longer.

Many of the caves of western Kentucky grew larger and larger until their roofs collapsed. Such collapses left holes, called sinkholes, at the surface. The nearly circular sinkholes of the area have filled with water and formed lakes. Sinkholes still form in limestone today. These may take people who live near them by surprise when they collapse suddenly.

Most of the water drainage of the Kentucky cave area is underground. As a result, few rivers are seen. Those that do appear at the surface often disappear under the ground. They may emerge again several miles away.

↶ A thick limestone deposit revealed by a roadcut

A river emerging from a limestone cavern ↷

9

Earth's Plates

Any look at a globe shows that some of Earth's continents seem to fit together like jigsaw pieces. Fossils matching across two or more continents show that the continents must once have been joined together.

Earth's **lithosphere** is the **crust** plus the top of the very thick layer called the **mantle**. The part of the mantle on which the crust "floats" is called the **asthenosphere**. Unlike the rest of the mantle, which is solid, the asthenosphere is slightly **molten**.

Scientists have found that the lithosphere is broken into twelve large and several smaller sections. These sections are called **tectonic plates**. *Tectonic* means "to build." The growth and movement of continents happen because of the activity that occurs at the boundaries between plates.

Tectonic plates are both pushed and pulled around on the mantle. They are pushed apart at undersea areas called **spreading ridges**.

*Tectonic plates are separated by spreading ridges (in red) and **subduction** zones (in yellow).*

NORTH AMERICAN PLATE

NORTH AMERICAN PLATE

EURASIAN PLATE

PACIFIC PLATE

JUAN DE FUCA PLATE

CARIBBEAN PLATE

ARABIAN PLATE

INDIAN PLATE

PHILIPPINE PLATE

Equator

Equator

Equator

COCOS PLATE

NAZCA PLATE

SOUTH AMERICAN PLATE

AFRICAN PLATE

AUSTRALIAN PLATE

PACIFIC PLATE

SCOTIA PLATE

ANTARCTIC PLATE

These ridges form a continuous line that twists and turns around the floor of the planet's oceans. Molten rock from the mantle rises at these ridges as **lava**. The lava hardens into rock and pushes apart the two plates that meet at a ridge. The new rock forms new ocean floor.

Elsewhere under the oceans seafloor is sucked back into the mantle for recycling. These places are called subduction zones. When seafloor is subducted, the two tectonic plates that meet at the zone are pulled closer together. One is forced under the other and back into the mantle.

Throughout Earth's history, spreading ridges and subduction zones have come and gone. The action has moved the tectonic plates around the planet. Sometimes the continents have drifted apart. Sometimes they have moved together, meeting in huge, mountain-building collisions. Today, the Atlantic Ocean is growing very slowly, an average of only about 1 inch (2.5 cm) a year. The Pacific Ocean is shrinking as slowly.

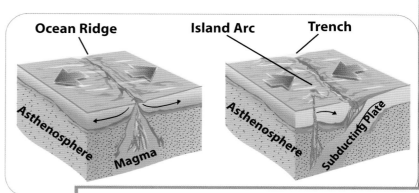

At the boundaries between tectonic plates, plates are either pushed apart (left) or pulled together (right).

The Moving Land

As the Carboniferous Period began, the continent of Laurentia was still considerably smaller than North America is today. The entire future western mountain region, from Alaska down into Mexico, had not yet **accreted**, or attached itself to the continent.

Laurentia lay across the equator with today's Arctic coast facing east instead of north. Attached to it at Greenland was another continent called **Baltica**. Throughout the late Paleozoic, events that affected Laurentia also affected Baltica. Together, Baltica and Laurentia are often called the continent of Laurussia (or Euramerica).

Baltica would someday separate from Laurentia again. It would eventually form the land of western Europe and part of Russia.

Most of the other continents were grouped into a giant **supercontinent** called **Gondwana**. It was located around the South Pole. Periodically, **glaciers** formed on these continents and then melted back. As the glaciers formed and retreated, sea level around the globe also changed. During warmer periods, sea level was high. Warm shallow seas then spread onto the lower lands of Laurentia and the other continents. The water that lay between Laurentia and Gondwana is called the Iapetus Ocean.

Living things made great evolutionary progress during these warm periods when there was so much shallow sea. Then, when the glaciers formed again, taking water from the ocean, these warm seas on the northern continents retreated back into the global ocean. Numerous life forms died off. Life on the continents was literally an ebb and flow in response to major climate changes.

↰ *Glaciers covered much of the southern supercontinent of Gondwana during the late Paleozoic. Antarctica, shown here, has similar glaciers today.*

12

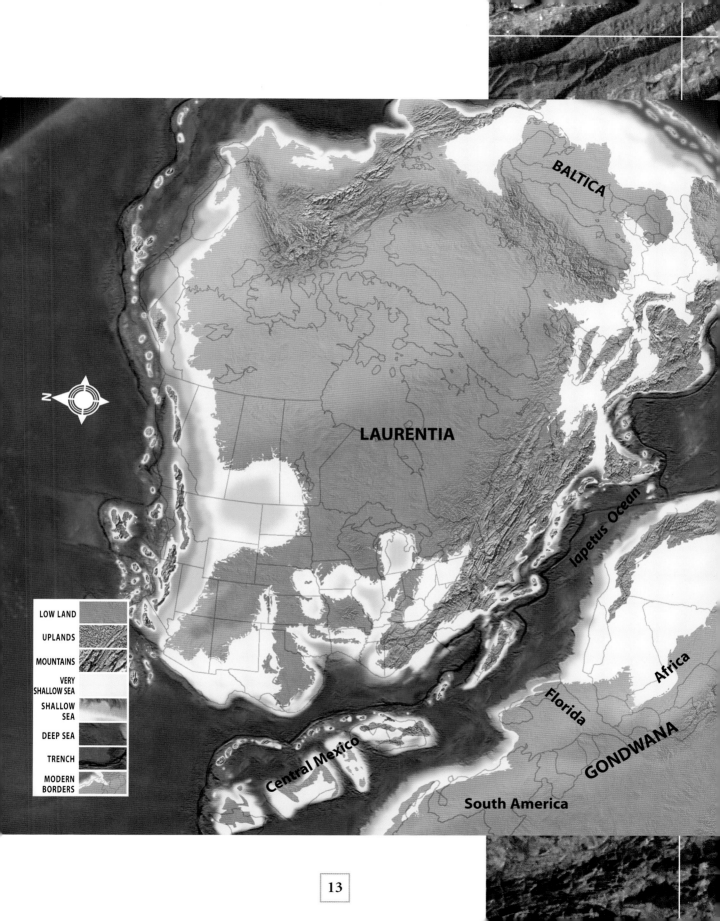

LOW LAND
UPLANDS
MOUNTAINS
VERY SHALLOW SEA
SHALLOW SEA
DEEP SEA
TRENCH
MODERN BORDERS

BALTICA

LAURENTIA

Iapetus Ocean

Florida

Africa

GONDWANA

Central Mexico

South America

Chapter 2

The Making of a Supercontinent

Early in the Devonian Period, perhaps 400 million years ago, a new warm, shallow sea began to spread across Laurentia. Called the Kaskaskia Sea, it covered much of the continent well into the Mississippian Epoch. Then it began to retreat.

Throughout this time, eroded sand and other materials settled to the bottom of the continental sea. This **sediment** was eventually covered. It was compressed into the **sedimentary rock** called sandstone. The Kaskaskia Sea retreated during the late Mississippian. These rocks then were exposed to erosion by wind and water. The eroded sand was recycled into more **sandstone** deposits.

During the Pennsylvanian Epoch, another sea arose, called the Absaroka Sea. *Absaroka* is the Native American name for the Crow tribe. The Absaroka was the fourth flood to occur during the Paleozoic. It did not cover as much of Laurentia as the Kaskaskia Sea had. There was still plenty of time, though, for sediments to build up before it began to retreat. The Absaroka Sea had retreated back into the ocean by the end of the Pennsylvanian Epoch. Several layers of rock in the Grand Canyon were deposited as sediment in the Absaroka Sea.

Vast layers of sedimentary rock built up during the flooding of the continent. These layers were eventually forced upward into mountains. This happened when one landmass collided with another in a huge event called an **orogeny**. Orogenies can be defined as mountain-building episodes in Earth's history.

↰ *Monument Valley in the Red Rock Country of the Arizona-Utah border is a creation of eroding red-colored sandstone.*

Unlike car collisions, continental collisions happen very slowly. But the effects can be amazing. The movement of continents during the late Paleozoic resulted in the biggest continent Earth has ever known. This was a single supercontinent called **Pangea** (also spelled *Pangaea*), meaning "all lands." When one landmass struck another during the formation of Pangea, mountains were built.

Constructing the Appalachians

The mountains that eventually formed the whole eastern portion of North America are the Appalachians. Today's mountains—or what remains of them—are actually the result of three different orogenies.

During an orogeny, rock is mangled and **deformed**. This happens as a result of forces such as **uplift**, **folding**, and **faulting**. Folding forces sedimentary layers into arches and dips. These are like waves on the ocean or the crumpling of a tablecloth being pushed on one end. Faulting breaks layers of rock and shifts one part away from the rock that it was previously touching. This rock deformation can take millions of years to happen. At the end of that time, the land that crashed into the continent has become attached, or accreted, to the continent, making it larger.

The first collision in the building of the Appalachians was the Taconic orogeny. It took place during the Ordovician Period, about 460 million years ago. It was caused by the small continent of Baltica crashing into Laurentia. It built mountains in New England and added land to what would become eastern Canada.

Pressure, such as from a collision, can make rock fold (top) or fault, meaning "break" (below). These pictures show what happened on a small scale. But the same kind of deformation on a large scale can build huge mountain ranges.

16

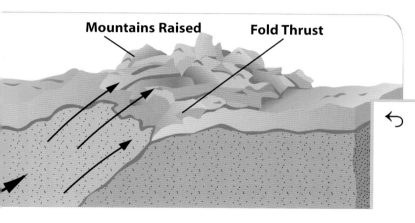

Mountains Raised   **Fold Thrust**

The collision of two continents resulted in the formation of large mountain ranges. On each side of the mountains, sedimentary rock could be moved long distances in fold thrusts.

The next round of mountain-building in the Appalachians is called the Acadian orogeny (called the Caledonian orogeny in Europe. It started in the late Devonian, about 400 million years ago. Over the next 50 million years, it added land called Avalonia between New York and Newfoundland. Some Laurentian land was subducted during the process. Many volcanoes formed west of Avalonia.

The landmass called **Siberia** also joined Baltica and Laurentia. Together, they formed a supercontinent that has been called Laurasia. Even with three continents making up Laurasia, it was not nearly as large as Gondwana in the south.

Gondwana Came Along

The North American continent was turned clockwise and was lying on its side along the equator. The giant Gondwana itself was now approaching Laurentia from the south.

From about 300 to 250 million years ago, during the Pennsylvanian and Permian, the portion of Gondwana that was made up of northwestern Africa crashed into Laurentia. Millions of years later, Africa disconnected from Laurentia during the breakup of Pangea. It left behind a chunk of land called the African **terrane**. A terrane is a piece of crust that has an entirely different geological history than the crust around it. The African terrane lay along the region that today extends from Connecticut to Georgia.

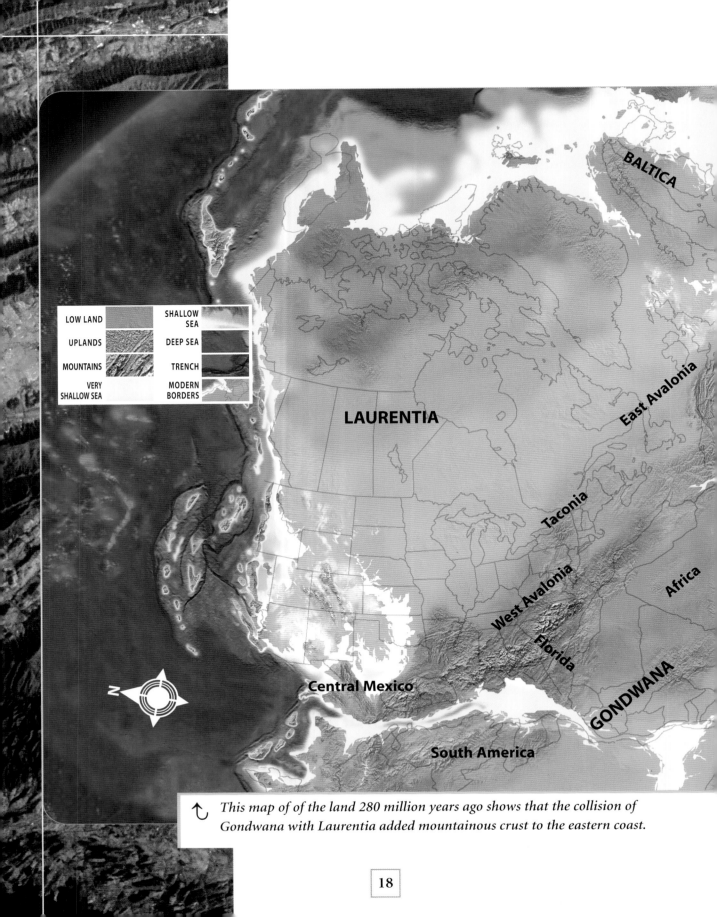

LOW LAND

UPLANDS

MOUNTAINS

VERY SHALLOW SEA

SHALLOW SEA

DEEP SEA

TRENCH

MODERN BORDERS

BALTICA

LAURENTIA

East Avalonia

Taconia

West Avalonia

Africa

Florida

Central Mexico

GONDWANA

South America

This map of of the land 280 million years ago shows that the collision of Gondwana with Laurentia added mountainous crust to the eastern coast.

Sedimentary rocks in the Ouachita Mountains in the southern Appalachians were turned on their sides by the collision with the African terrane. ↺

Gondwana was rotating as it collided with Laurentia. This caused a series of collisions rather than one massive one. The largest was the Alleghenian orogeny. It built mountains from Britain (which, as part of Baltica, was close to Greenland at that time) through Newfoundland, and south into the southern Appalachians. Huge beds of ancient sediments and volcanic lava were thrust up.

Sediments were also building up along the southern coast of Laurentia. These began to settle in deep water before the Mississippian Epoch. The deposits built up further during the Pennsylvanian.

As eastern Laurentia was being bumped by Africa, the Gulf Coast was colliding with the northern coast of South America, which, like Africa, was also part of Gondwana. The collision formed mountains called the Ouachitas of Arkansas and Oklahoma. These mountains are regarded as part of the southern Appalachian chain.

The joining of Gondwana to Laurentia was the last big event creating the supercontinent of Pangea. It had taken almost 100 million years to form. All the major continents of the planet were now attached to each other. They would remain that way until they started to break up during the middle Mesozoic. The dinosaurs that lived during the first part of the Mesozoic Era were free to wander across the face of the largest continent the world has ever known.

↺ *Several orogenies, shown in different colors, built eastern North America.*

Looking at the Smokies

The Smoky Mountains are part of the southern Appalachians. An uplift occurred there about 200 million years ago. It was caused by the collision of continents in the Alleghenian orogeny. Forces of the collision thrust much of the rock upward into tilted layers. Folding can be seen, and some of the rock has been broken, or fractured, and faulted.

Almost all of the rocks in the Smokies are of Precambrian age. The oldest of them are **granite**, **schist**, and **gneiss**. The younger of the Precambrian rocks are sedimentary. Many of the highest peaks are made of **quartzite**. This rock is resistant to **weathering**.

The valleys are V-shaped. The shape indicates that streams are the principal means of erosion. By contrast, glaciers tend to smooth out the land and make U-shaped valleys. Here, the ridges are more rounded than the jagged mountains of western North America. The rounding is due to greater amount of weathering that occurs in this warm and humid climate. The land throughout the area has been scarred by past landslides, as in the photograph.

Mountain Building Spreads Westward

Mountain-building collisions did not just uplift sedimentary rock into mountains. Great pressure was created by these collisions. This pressure could also thrust huge regions of rock inland. One massive thrust of rock moved what had been Laurentia's coast inland over other rock. This slab of rock was an average of 6 miles (9.6 km) thick. Incredibly, it was moved 162 miles (260 km) inland.

The slab was then compressed further into a series of folds running from the land that became New York to Alabama. The folded region is called the Valley and Ridge **Province** of eastern North America. It looks rather like a series of waves on the sea or a crumpled blanket. The Pennsylvanian coal beds are part of this Valley and Ridge Province.

The forces creating the Appalachians didn't stop on the east coast. They could be felt all the way across the continent. The entire region that would someday become the Rocky Mountains was lifted up. The region, called the Ancestral Rockies, was not yet the massive peaks we know today. This uplifted area of rocks of Pennsylvanian origin gradually eroded. The result of the erosion is the red sandstone that makes much of western North America so colorful. A good example is Monument Valley, which lies along the Arizona-Utah border.

The Valley and Ridge Province lies west of the Appalachian Mountains. It consists of a series of great folds of rock that have eroded, filling in the valleys between with sediment.

Red Rocks of Monument Valley

Monument Valley is a Navajo Tribal Park along the Arizona-Utah border. Some of the most colorful rocks on Earth are seen here and in the surrounding region. The entire region is called Red Rock Country because of the intense color of the sandstone.

The red color is caused primarily by the iron content of the rock. Compounds of iron are not so much in the grains of sand. Instead, they are in the "cement" that holds the grains together. Crystals of the mineral iron oxide lie between the grains and wrap around them. Iron oxide is also known as rust. It is formed in water when oxygen and iron atoms join to form molecules.

In the Monument Valley region and elsewhere in southeastern Utah, thick beds of red Permian sandstone form towering landforms. The outstanding rock formations of this region are the remains of a once-higher **plateau**. The plateau is now in the late stages of erosion. The dry climate helps form steep profiles in the landscape. Similar landforms in a more humid climate would have a more rounded form.

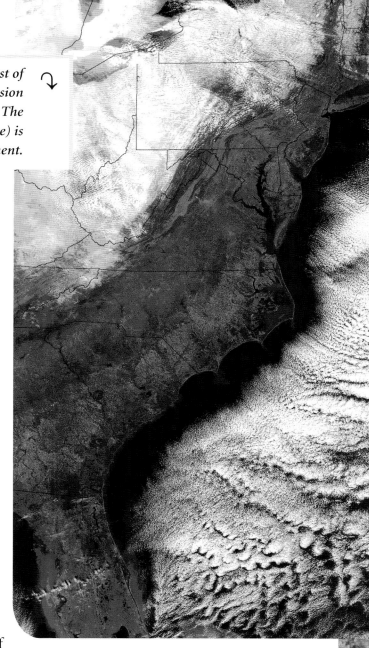

The higher land away from the southeastern coast of the United States was the result of the last collision that assembled the supercontinent of Pangea. The lower land along the coast (seen here from space) is the Coastal Plain, which was built of sediment.

Pulling Together Pangea

Meanwhile, the part of Gondwana that would become Africa was approaching Laurentia's coast from the south. It may be that additional land was caught in between Africa and Laurentia. This land later became the Piedmont area. The Piedmont lies between the mountains and the Coastal Plain of the east coast. Once the two continents struck, the supercontinent of Pangea was basically complete. It would last 100 million years.

By the end of the Paleozoic, Pangea's landmass stretched all the way from the North Pole to the South Pole. A single planet-wide ocean, called the Panthalassa Ocean, surrounded Pangea.

The future continent of North America was still tropical. It lay at the middle of the western side of the supercontinent. The southern part of Pangea, which had been Gondwana in earlier times, was still covered by a huge ice cap. The glaciers were beginning to retreat, however. This happened as Gondwana moved northward into warmer areas.

Geologists are not completely certain of the structure of Pangea at the end of the Paleozoic. It was probably like a huge C. The main debate concerns the exact position of South America within the landmasses making up the supercontinent.

Pangea probably existed from 300 to 200 million years ago. During most of that period, subduction zones surrounded the supercontinent. The seafloor of the ocean surrounding Pangea was drawn down into the mantle. Any small bits of land riding above the subduction zone or any volcanoes that formed around them was pushed toward continental margins. This land often became attached to the growing supercontinent.

The name *Pangea* means "all lands." This supercontinent didn't really include all landmasses of the planet, however. As you can see on the adjacent global map, several smaller chunks of land remained separated. These would eventually be included in the continent of Asia.

Because the continents were now gathered into a new supercontinent, there was less coastal area that could be occupied by warm shallow seas. During most of the Paleozoic, marine life evolved in the seas.

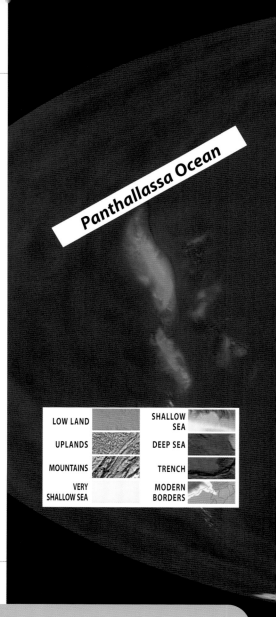

Panthallassa Ocean

LOW LAND	SHALLOW SEA
UPLANDS	DEEP SEA
MOUNTAINS	TRENCH
VERY SHALLOW SEA	MODERN BORDERS

At Work in Limestone Caves

Broad, level beds of limestone were deposited during the Pennsylvanian Epoch in the region around Kansas City, Missouri. Today, these limestone beds provide natural underground storage—and even living space. For almost a hundred years, the limestone was mined as a construction material. Chambers were dug that have now been turned into massive and inexpensive storage space. The temperature is quite constant—a pleasant 65°F (18°C). Rains and snows don't penetrate the chambers. The largest tenant of the limestone chambers is the U.S. Postal Service.

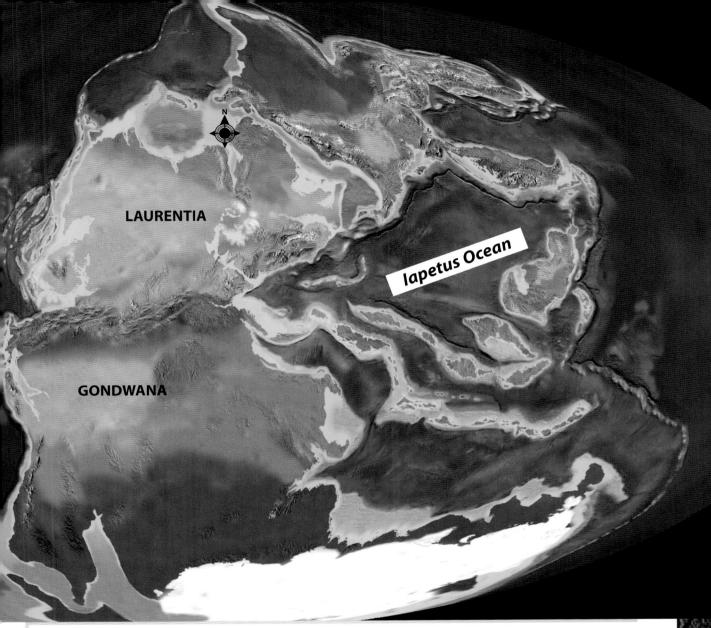

The supercontinent Pangea stretched from the North Pole to the South Pole by the end of the Paleozoic Era. The Alleghenian orogeny built the mountains visible along the equator, where Laurentia and Gondwana were joined for 100 million years. Laurentia lay to the north.

Great quantities of limestone were deposited then as well. However, during the late Paleozoic, there was less area covered by the shallow seas. With less sea area, there were fewer algae and shelled animals to make limestone. As a result, paleontologists have found fewer fossils in the late Paleozoic limestone.

The West

The western region of North America is called the **Cordillera**. The name comes from the Spanish word for "rope." Going east to west, the Cordillera runs from central Colorado at the east face of the Rocky Mountains to the Pacific Ocean. From north to south, it runs from the top of Alaska to the bottom of Mexico. The Rockies make up the largest mountain chain in the Cordillera. But they are not alone. Several mountain ranges in addition to the Rockies in the Cordillera were formed at different times.

Some of the most spectacular sedimentary rocks were deposited along the western regions of the continent. These rocks were uplifted into mountains and eventually eroded into wonderful shapes. These later became part of the Canadian Rockies. The Burgess Shale, which is a fossil bed in early Paleozoic rock, is part of this same development. It reveals much about the earliest living things made up of more than one cell.

Earlier in the Paleozoic, western Laurentia was submerged in the ocean. For millions of years, huge deposits of sand and limestone accumulated on the submerged portion. This portion is called the coastal shelf. It was much like the eastern margin of North America today.

A museum exhibit shows some of the living things found as fossils in the Burgess Shale of the Canadian Rockies.

The Canadian Rocky Mountains, shown here at Banff in Alberta, were built when great sheets of Paleozoic rock were thrust upward by colliding landmasses.

The Cordilleran Region, or belt, began to be developed during the late Paleozoic. The region first formed during early mountain-building episodes, or orogenies. These orogenies would eventually form the entire western part of North America. It began with the Antler orogeny.

The landmass referred to as Antler was formed as an **island arc**. Such a landmass is a collection of volcanoes that form along a subduction zone. Because the surface of Earth is curved, the volcanoes form a curve, or arc. The Antler island arc probably formed somewhere on the edge of a tectonic plate during the Devonian Period.

As the Pacific plate moved toward the North American plate, it carried the volcanic landmass with it. It also picked up some of the sediment on the coastal shelf. The plate carried the sediment toward the western edge of Laurentia. That edge of the continent was approximately in Utah at the time. During the Mississippian, the Antler arc was accreted to Laurentia. It formed land that stretched from the California-Nevada border through central Nevada into Idaho.

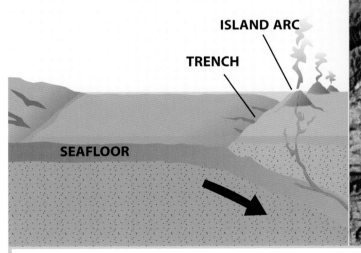

ISLAND ARC

TRENCH

SEAFLOOR

An island arc forms above an area where seafloor is subducting into a trench.

Chapter 3

Evolution: Life Taking over the Land

Many forms of living things were in trouble as the Mississippian Epoch started. A mass extinction of many species took place at the end of the Devonian, 350 million years ago. Some marine animals became extinct because there were fewer things to eat. The many kinds of seafloor creatures called trilobites, for example, were no longer available as a food source for other marine animals. Some species died out. As a result, other creatures were able to take advantage of living space that had been left unoccupied.

The Reef-Builders

One of the features of the ancient shallow seas was the formation of **reefs**. Reefs are stony structures made up of the accumulated calcium carbonate shells of sponges, **bryozoans**, and corals. Reefs provided homes for many other animals. This is because they could count on finding food sources there. The animals also could use the rough structures to hide from predators. Two huge groups of corals helped form the reefs throughout North America. These became extinct at the end of the Permian.

Laurentia was lying on its side at the time. The reef area stretched along the equator. Eventually, reefs turn into limestone rock. Huge limestone reefs covered most of North America from the southern United States to northern Alaska during the late Paleozoic. For example, a layer of the Grand Canyon is reef-formed limestone that formed during the Mississippian. It is called the Redwall Limestone.

↰ *Two **reptiles** of the Permian Period in a museum painting*

Reef Limestone of Carlsbad Caverns

Carlsbad Caverns are located in southeastern New Mexico. This cave system formed in reef limestone that developed during the Permian. However, unlike later reefs, this limestone was not made by coral skeletons. Instead, such creatures as sponges and algae formed it. Living reefs tend to be unstable structures. Large blocks break off and become embedded in the new growth. The resulting limestone of the caverns appears as a jumbled mass. There is little obvious sign of layering.

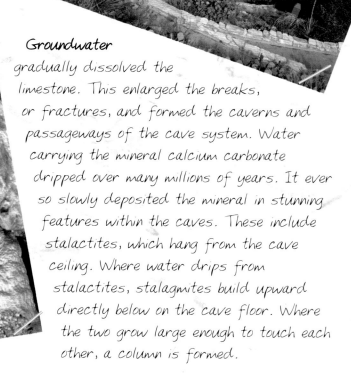

Groundwater gradually dissolved the limestone. This enlarged the breaks, or fractures, and formed the caverns and passageways of the cave system. Water carrying the mineral calcium carbonate dripped over many millions of years. It ever so slowly deposited the mineral in stunning features within the caves. These include stalactites, which hang from the cave ceiling. Where water drips from stalactites, stalagmites build upward directly below on the cave floor. Where the two grow large enough to touch each other, a column is formed.

Among the most common limestone-forming animals are the almost microscopic single-celled creatures called **foraminiferans**, or forams. Foram shells made up most of the sediment that accumulated on the seafloor during the late Carboniferous and the Permian. These single-celled organisms are enclosed in shells called tests. The tests were made of organic compounds, cemented sediment, or calcium carbonate. The many species had a wide variety of external shapes and internal structures.

Each species of foram existed for a geologically short period of time. It would be found worldwide in a particular marine environment. Later it was replaced by a new species. Forams make excellent **index fossils**.

↱ *Tiny foraminferan shells on an American dime*

Predators of the Sea

Many marine animals were a great deal larger than the forams. Two main types of large marine predators were prominent during the Permian. They were both cephalopods, ancestral groups of **mollusks** related to the nautilus and the octopus.

The fossil group called **ammonoids** fascinated the early explorers. They had discovered rocky versions of these curled creatures. They called the fossils snakestones and figured they were a "prank of nature." It wasn't until 1829 that the living version of coiled snakestones was discovered. The chambered nautilus was found to resemble the ancient fossils.

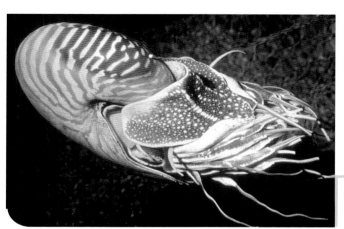

↰ *Today's chambered nautilus is the only descendant of the Paleozoic ammonoids.*

Looking at Cephalopods

Cephalopods are marine animals having a head surrounded by tentacles. Cephalopod fossils vary greatly in size. They range from a few inches to over 12 feet (3.6 m) in length. Some are straight and cone-shaped, while others are coiled.

Their shells are divided into a series of chambers, like rooms in a house. The chambers are separated by partitions, or walls. The soft-bodied animal lives in the last chamber. The other chambers are filled with air. This increases the buoyancy, or "floatability," of the animal.

Indentations called suture lines appear where the chambers' partitions join the wall of the shell. These sutures are useful in identifying species of cephalopods. On cephalopods from the Paleozoic Era, for example, the sutures are straight or only slightly curved. Later, during the Mesozoic Era, the sutures became very complex and crinkled.

↰ A cutaway of a coiled cephalopod, showing the chambers

↰ Suture lines visible on the outside of the shell

↰ Complex chambers in a noncoiled cephalopod

All the major types of fish were swimming the seas of the world by the end of the Devonian. One type, the jawless fish, failed to survive the Devonian Extinction. The other two kinds are those with skeletons of bone and those with skeletons of cartilage, which is the material that forms the human nose. These fish survive to this day. Bony fish evolved in freshwater during the Devonian. During the later Paleozoic, they also returned to the saltwater seas. The cartilaginous fish have skeletons made of the tough but flexible cartilage. They have always been marine species. Today, the only cartilaginous fish are sharks and rays.

Today's sharks are the descendants of some of the oldest fish, those with a skeleton of cartilage instead of bone. ↱

Shark Scales and Teeth

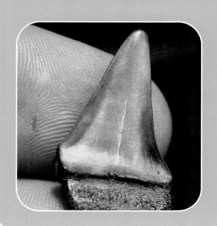

Fossil shark scales are the most abundant of all vertebrate fossils. However, they are very small. Many fossil hunters never notice them at all. They are more likely to see fossil shark teeth, which are much larger, such as the one shown at the left. One type of shark, called the xenacanth shark, had teeth with a double prong on them. The xenacanth had a long spike on its head. Shaped like a large eel, it was an important predator of Permian seas.

Plants on Land

The second part of the Paleozoic began 354 million years ago. It began with a huge increase in the number of plants that could survive on land. These plants did not just survive—thrived and diversified, or developed more variety. Among the groups that were evolving were club mosses, ferns, horsetails, and even seed plants.

The club mosses and their relatives are called **lycopods**. Today, they are found as little ground-hugging spiky plants. These small plants have shoots that spread underground. During the Mississippian, however, they grew into trees. One lycopod, called the scale tree, was an important part of the swamp life that became coal in eastern Laurentia. Such trees were the first widespread use of a **vascular** system in plants. This system allowed plants to grow tall because water could reach all the way from the ground to the top. The water traveled through tubes called veins.

The trunk of a Pennsylvanian scale tree, or lycopod. Fossilized branches of a lycopod are shown below.

The scale trees were probably the most important producers of coal. These trees grew to a height of more than 100 feet (30 m). They had long, straight trunks. Lycopods usually reproduced by means of small bodies called **spores**. These were enclosed in cases on the ends of the branches. There were only a few branches. The branches were generally located near the top of the tree. The tree's leaves emerged from the branches and from the trunk. When the leaves fell off, the places where they had been attached left a pattern of scars, called scales, on the trunk.

Coal-Making Sphenopsids

A group of plants called sphenopsids are known today only for the little horsetails, or scouring rushes. But their ancient ancestors contributed greatly to the coal we use today. Most sphenopsids became almost extinct after the Paleozoic.

Sphenopsids—then and now—are recognizable by the branches or leaves that spread out in a whorl at joints going up the stem. The reproductive spores are found at the top of the stem. Their stems did not branch, and they were slender with vertical ribs.

Today's horsetails are small plants. During the Pennsylvanian, they reached heights of about 100 feet (30 m). The most prominent trees in coal forests belonged to a group called calamites. They were hardy and kept on growing even as sediment filled in around them.

↑ A sphenopsid, or horsetail, tree from the Paleozoic

↘ Fossil imprint of sphenopsid leaves

Today's horsetail ↻

The Time of the Ferns

The sphenopsids may have led to the ferns. These are much more familiar today, especially in rainforest areas. Ferns were so common during the Carboniferous that the Pennsylvanian has been called the "Age of Ferns."

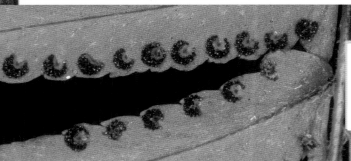

Ferns, old and new:
Fronds, or leaf branches, of today's tree fern (top left)
Fossilized fern fronds, found in Antarctica (top right)
Reproductive spores on fern leaves (left)

Ferns thrived in a moist, warm atmosphere. This atmosphere prevailed at the time in Laurentia. Ferns were the main developers of leaves. The leaves were a means of expanding a plant's exposure to sunlight. They supported the plant's ability to carry on **photosynthesis**. The leaves had to have pores, or openings, in their surfaces. The pores took in carbon dioxide and released oxygen. Like club mosses and horsetails, ferns bear little specks on their leaves called spores. Spores are reproductive structures. They grow exposed on the leaves instead of encased in a hard covering like a seed.

Ferns provided a great deal of the bulk of the plant matter that turned into coal. Fossil ferns are often found in the flat **shale** formed in coal beds.

A different group of plants called seed ferns developed. These looked like ferns, but, unlike ferns, they produced seeds instead of spores for reproduction. Seeds must be fertilized by pollen to grow. Seeds became the most important means of plant reproduction. Seed ferns themselves disappeared in the Permian Extinction.

Museum reproduction of a seed fern from the Pennsylvanian Epoch

Modern cycads have changed little since they developed during the Permian.

The planet's climate began to change in the Permian. As a result, many warmth-loving plants disappeared. Ferns were replaced in their great abundance by **cycads**. These produced coal, but not in the huge quantities that plants did in the previous periods.

The planet was cooler and drier, so cycads did not grow as tall as the previous coal-makers. The cycads had woody stems that ended on top with a palm-like spray of leaves. A few cycads still grow in Florida and Mexico. They look rather like pineapples.

Insects

Moving through the forests of the late Paleozoic were insects and other **arthropods**. They reached huge sizes never seen since. During the Carboniferous, these animals were able to grow to giant sizes for several reasons. They had no natural enemies that could prevent them from growing. There was much more oxygen in the atmosphere than there is now. During this period, there was perhaps as much as 35 percent oxygen, compared to today's 18 percent.

During the early Pennsylvanian, flying insects with fixed wings evolved. A giant dragonfly is shown on page 49. By the end of that epoch, wings that could be folded had evolved. Insects with foldable wings had a special advantage. They could go into tiny places for food. Fixed-wing insects were limited to feeding in the open.

Other insects such as cockroaches scurried among the rotting vegetation at the base of the trees. A giant millipede of the time measured more than 6.5 feet (2 m) long and 6 inches (15 cm) wide. It was so big that it has been labeled "Godzillapede," after the giant movie monster.

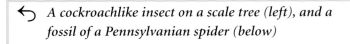
↩ *A cockroachlike insect on a scale tree (left), and a fossil of a Pennsylvanian spider (below)*

As the late Paleozoic started, some specialized fish developed the ability to survive on land. They became **amphibians**—four-footed land animals tied to the water, such as Amphibiamus (inset).

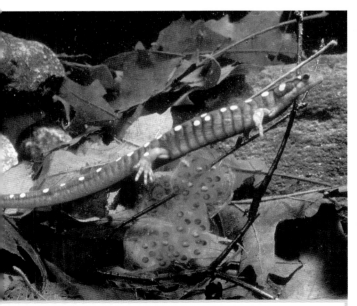

Adult amphibians like this salamander can live on land much of the time, but they must return to water to lay their eggs.

Amphibians

Amphibians got their start during the Devonian. During this period, some fish developed in ways that helped them move around on land. Certain gills, which are organs that have the ability to take oxygen from water, changed into lungs. Lungs could utilize oxygen taken from the atmosphere instead of from the water.

These first amphibians also developed bones in their side fins. With bones, these fins were strong enough to support the animals' weight on land, without the help of water. A whole new kind of animal had evolved.

Amphibians of the Late Paleozoic

Fossil evidence indicates that amphibians probably evolved from fish that moved onto land, except to reproduce. Today's typical amphibian still spends most of its adult life on land. It then returns to water to lay its fishlike eggs. The eggs develop into a young form called **larvae**. These young use gills for respiration, or breathing. The larvae gradually develop into adult forms that breathe through lungs. An adult amphibian's limbs sprawl out sideways rather than standing upright. As a result, it barely holds its body above the ground.

Labyrinthodonts were a group of amphibians that lived in the swamps of the Carboniferous. They are named for a kind of maze (or labyrinth) pattern in their teeth. One called Eryops was bulky and had a flattish skull. Its jaw contained cone-shaped teeth. The skeleton of this large amphibian shows that it walked with its knees bent outward. It probably had an awkward, slow way of walking.

↩ Eryops

Another labyrinthodont
amphibian, Trematops ↪

During the Mississippian, amphibians took over most damp environments on Laurentia. The land was theirs. But they had to stay near water to reproduce. Amphibians laid their eggs in water. Their larvae, called tadpoles, had to live in water until they gradually transformed into land-living adults.

Some amphibians grew to great sizes. The anthracosaur was shaped like a crocodile and reached 13 feet (4 m) long.

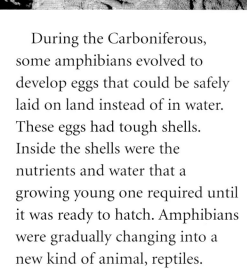

Cacops and its relatives were common amphibians during the Carboniferous and Permian. A fossil like this one (top) was used by scientists to create a model (bottom). ↱

A pine snake in the process of hatching from its land-based eggs. Such eggs provided the young reptiles all the nutrients and safety they needed. ↰

During the Carboniferous, some amphibians evolved to develop eggs that could be safely laid on land instead of in water. These eggs had tough shells. Inside the shells were the nutrients and water that a growing young one required until it was ready to hatch. Amphibians were gradually changing into a new kind of animal, reptiles.

The Earliest Reptile Fossil

In the late 1990s, an amateur fossil collector found the remains of a four-footed creature in Scotland. It was possibly the first known reptile. The remains date to about 340 million years ago, during the Mississippian. It is the oldest fossil found of an animal that clearly lived on land.

A chameleon hatching from its egg. When reptiles hatch, they are ready to go. They do not go through an immature larval stage, as amphibians do.

Reptiles

At Joggins, Nova Scotia, in 1851, one of the world's oldest reptile fossils was found inside the fossilized hollow trunks of lycopod trees. Its discoverers, Sir Charles Lyell and Sir William Dawson, were among the founders of **paleontology** as a science. Their find at Joggins provided the first evidence that animals that were strictly land dwellers had been alive during the Mississippian.

Dawson suggested that perhaps the lycopod trees had broken off and sediment settled around the broken trunks. This continued until the new soil layers reached to the top of the broken trunk. Then, reptile after reptile unsuspectingly fell into the hollow trunk and could not get out again. More recent studies, however, suggest that these oldest of reptiles were not really trapped in the sediment. Instead, they may actually have lived in the hollow stumps.

Reptiles gradually evolved into different groups. These groups took advantage of different environments. One group, called the archosaurs (meaning "ruling reptiles"), was just getting started during the Permian. They eventually became the ancestors of the Mesozoic dinosaurs. Others arose that could survive in hot, dry climates. These became today's turtles, lizards, snakes, and crocodiles.

Examples of today's reptiles: common garter snake (above left), American alligator (right), horned lizard (below left), and snapping turtle (right)

Field Note

Reptiles of the Late Paleozoic

Unlike amphibians, reptiles did not need to live near bodies of water in order to reproduce and develop. They laid eggs with hard shells. These eggs could keep enough water and food for the developing unhatched young as well as protect it. The young passed through larval stages within the egg. It then hatched as a miniature version of the adult.

Seymoria fossils were found in the Permian sediments of Texas. These fossils possessed characteristics of a primitive reptile. The skeletons appear to be those of a transition between amphibian and reptile.

Cynognathus was a mammal-like reptile. Such reptiles had legs that developed more vertically beneath the body, rather than sprawling sideways. Unlike most reptiles, their teeth were more specialized. They showed development of incisors, canines, and cheek teeth.

The kangaroo of Australia is a marsupial. The female gives birth to a very undeveloped baby, which she then carries in a pouch on her stomach.

Marsupials

Unlike the animals that became dinosaurs and today's reptiles, another group evolved from amphibians in a different way during the late Paleozoic. They became able to withstand cool, even cold, climates. They did this by developing hair instead of scales. They also laid their eggs in pouches on the mother's stomach where the eggs could develop protected from weather.

These just-born babies of the American opossum (below) could not survive if they were not immediately transferred to the mother's warm pouch, where they develop.

Few fossils of these earliest **mammals**, called **marsupials**, have been found. They apparently developed in Asia. They then made their way to Laurentia. Today, marsupials are found primarily in Australia. There is only one marsupial still living in North America. It is the American opossum.

Edaphosaurus was an early Permian fin-backed reptile like Dimetrodon, *which is shown on page 63. Larger than* Dimetrodon, Edaphosaurus *could reach 11 feet (3.3 m).*

The First Monstrous Land Animals

By the Permian, animals of various kinds were thriving in land environments. Some of these land animals became quite huge.

Dimetrodon, or finback, was a large flesh-eater. It had a huge fin, or "sail," on its back. The sail may have been used as a cooling radiator and a heat collector. Actually, no one really knows what it was for. When seen in a museum, people often mistake this 6-foot (2-m) animal for a dinosaur. However, it lived much earlier than dinosaurs, during the late Carboniferous and early Permian.

Dimetrodon was an early ancestor of mammals. It was one of the earliest of a category of animals called **synapsids**. The animals in this category have a synapse, or hole, in the skull. Around the synapse were anchored muscles that controlled the jaw. Today's mammals still have that feature.

Finback is the most famous of the synapsids called pelycosaurs. These had features that were both reptile-like and mammal-like. The pelycosaurs were an in-between group of animals.

The early synapsids gave way by the end of the Permian to the advanced synapsids. These were even closer to mammals. *Tetraceratops* (no relation to the dinosaur *Triceratops*) was a large salamander-looking animal of the late Permian. *Estemmenosuchus* was a synapsid that could appear ferocious. This was because it was about 12 feet (3.6 m) long and stood 6 feet (1.8 m) high. But it was a mild plant-eater that could eat tough plants with its strong teeth. Fossils of these animals were found in Russia. Since Siberia was attached to Laurentia at the time, they probably also lived in North America.

Mammals remained fairly insignificant during the next era, the Mesozoic. The central part of Pangea was huge and far from the ocean. As a result, the climate was blazingly hot and searingly dry. This kind of climate encouraged the development of reptiles over mammals. The Mesozoic would become known as the "Age of Dinosaurs." But after dinosaurs became extinct, mammals would come into their own.

↩ *Plant-eating reptiles of the Paleozoic, like this pelycosaur, may have been related to the plant-eating dinosaurs that arose later.*

Chapter 4

Coal:
Future Fuel

For almost three hundred years, industrial nations have depended on the black or brown rock called coal. It is burned for heat and for energy to make electricity and power machines.

Coal is one of the main **fossil fuels**. These are materials produced by heat and pressure within the earth. The others are petroleum and natural gas. The process of making coal within the earth began more than 350 million years ago.

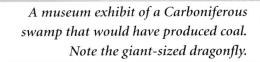

A museum exhibit of a Carboniferous ↱
swamp that would have produced coal.
Note the giant-sized dragonfly.

Coal can be defined as carbon-rich burnable rock. It contains more than 50 percent carbon. When carbon combines with oxygen, the process is called burning, or combustion. The products of combustion are heat, light, and the gas carbon dioxide.

The plants that turned into coal grew in swamps. Scientists suggest that the swamps were similar to today's Florida Everglades. The swamp water contained little oxygen. As a result, when the huge trees of the coal forests died, they fell into water and did not rot.

If oxygen had been available, the carbon would have combined with it. It would have made the gas carbon dioxide. Instead, the stems of the trees and ferns turned soft and fibrous. Bacteria that do not require oxygen or produce carbon dioxide digested this material.

The swamps of today's Florida Everglades have the same low-oxygen water as coal swamps of the late Paleozoic. ↷

STAGES *and* TYPES *of* COAL

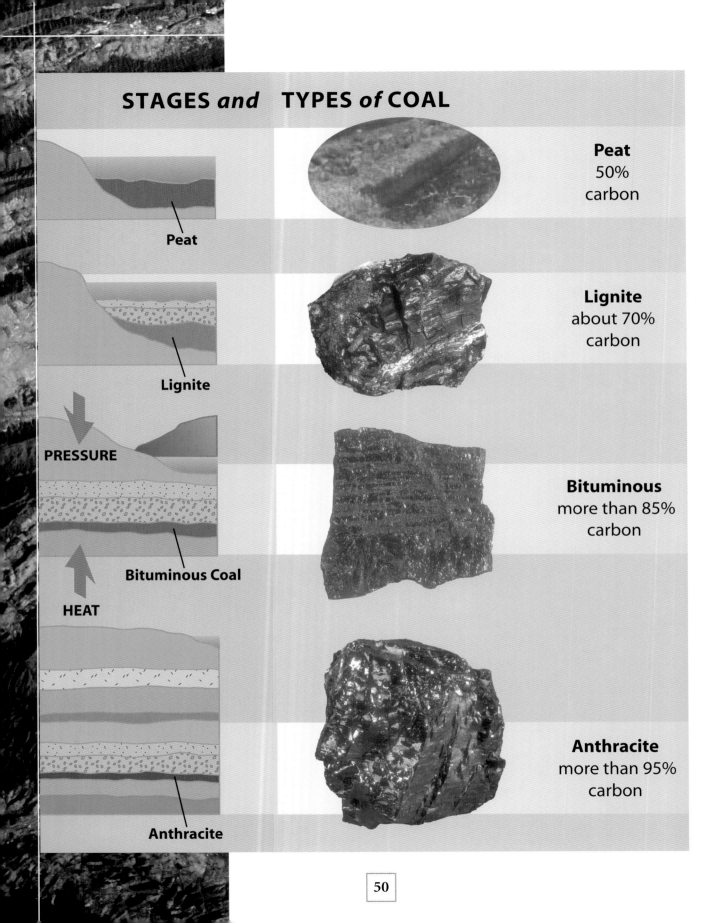

Peat
50% carbon

Lignite
about 70% carbon

Bituminous
more than 85% carbon

Anthracite
more than 95% carbon

Peat

Lignite

PRESSURE

Bituminous Coal

HEAT

Anthracite

50

The delta of the Sacramento River in California is a huge, flat area of peat soil. Much of it has been drained and turned into productive farmland.

The carbon content of the plants was not lost. Such partially digested material is collected today and burned for fuel as **peat**. Peat is still being made wherever boggy, or wet, swampy ground exists. Such places exist in Scotland, large parts of Canada, and the Okefenokee Swamp of Georgia.

Over time, sediments accumulated on top of the peat. The weight of the additional material compacted the peat. This forced any remaining water and gases from it. The material had become **lignite**, or brown coal. Lignite had changed so little that it still contained recognizable plant parts.

Lignite was compressed further, making what is called **bituminous**, or soft coal. Over many millions more years, the coal was pressed down further by additional weight on it. It turned into the hardest coal, called **anthracite**, or black or hard coal.

Each stage in coal making is usable. Only anthracite is very efficient at producing heat, however.

It is estimated that every 1 foot (30 cm) of coal required a layer of plant debris at least 6 feet (1.8 m) thick.

Making Red Rock Instead of Coal

A great deal of carbon was hidden away when coal was laid down during the Carboniferous Period. Ordinarily, that carbon would have contributed to carbon dioxide in the atmosphere. Some scientists think that the extra oxygen in the atmosphere reacted with iron instead of carbon. The result was a buildup of the compound iron oxide. This compound is red (rust) in color. Rock formed during the Permian is generally red because it contains iron oxide.

Coal Deposits

Many coal-making plants were available during the Paleozoic. As a result, coal is abundant around the planet today. The greatest coal beds are located on the continents that were in tropical regions or farther north during this part of the Paleozoic. The largest deposits are in the United States, China, and Russia. Europe also has some major deposits.

Coal is a rock. Like all rocks, it is subject to folding and faulting. For example, anthracite coal does not lie in nice, easy-to-get-at layers. Coal deposits are called seams. Mining a deep, folded coal seam can be dangerous because miners and machines must work deep underground.

The quality of the fuel that lies within the earth ranges from the lowest grade peat, to lignite, bituminous, and anthracite. Each is found progressively deeper. The higher grades have a higher carbon content, glossier luster, and higher density. They also produce more heat energy when burned. Only about 2 percent of the coal mined in the United States is the highest grade, anthracite.

The North American anthracite coal deposited during the Pennsylvanian is found in a belt that is about 500 to 620 miles (800 to 1,000 km) wide. It lies mostly in a thick belt parallel to the Appalachian Mountains. The region was probably a swampy coastal plain at the time. It was located between the rising mountains and a shallow sea. These seas did not drain into the ocean until early in the Permian.

Pennsylvania's coal beds gave its name to the Pennsylvanian Epoch. The area was subjected to regular heavy rains, similar to today's monsoons in Asia. This additional water kept the forests in a jungle-like condition. The beds are often more than 40 feet (12 m) deep and cover thousands of square feet.

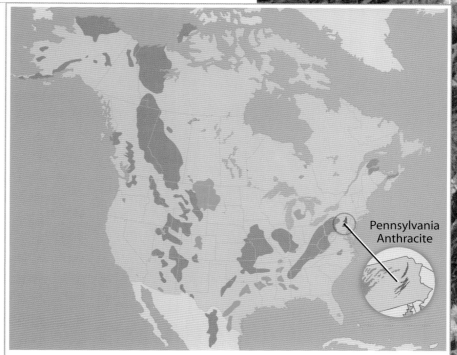

Pennsylvania Anthracite

■ **Anthracite**
■ **Bituminous**
■ **Lignite**

Heavy machinery and many workers ↱
may be used to mine anthracite coal
that is hundreds of feet underground.

While coal was being laid down in eastern North America, the central part of the continent was still collecting limestone. This indicates that it was under water. But as the shallow sea drained away, great swamps were left. They produced bituminous coal. Bituminous coal lies mostly in the Midwest, in Illinois, Iowa, and Missouri, as well as the near west. The plants forming it lived during the Permian Period.

Coal beds were also deposited during the Mesozoic Era. Most coal found in the western parts of North America was laid down in the Permian, the Mesozoic, and even into the Cenozoic. Wyoming is now the largest producer of coal in the United States. Its coal was not laid down until the late Mesozoic Era. This is when dinosaurs inhabited the swamps where it was formed.

In Canada, hard Pennsylvanian coals are found in Nova Scotia and New Brunswick. Some of the deposits extend out into the Atlantic under the ocean floor. Northwestern Canada has beds of bituminous coal. These beds were formed even before the Carboniferous, in the Devonian.

Wyoming is the largest producer of U.S. coal. Here, bituminous coal is being removed from the surface, which is called strip mining.

↱ A museum painting of a dying Carboniferous
swamp. A Dimetrodon is in the background.

Plants of the Coal Forest

The coal forests of the late Paleozoic were generally found in swampy areas. These areas were warm and had abundant rainfall. Today in North America, those conditions are most similar to subtropical coastal swamps such as those in Florida's Everglades. Lycopods, or scale trees, were the primary trees of the coal forests. Large sphenopsids, similar to today's smaller horsetails, were also found there.

The seed ferns had fernlike leaves. They reproduced by seeds, rather than spores, however. True ferns grew alongside them, but they carried spores on the underside of their leaves. Primitive **conifers** were also abundant.

Coal-Making Plants

As in the Devonian coal of Canada, a few coal beds were laid down before the Carboniferous. But it wasn't until about 325 million years ago that coal making began in earnest. At that time, there was regularly enough dead plant material available to deposit the deep beds needed for coal.

The major coal-maker in Laurentia was the club moss family. It has been estimated that 80 percent of North America's coal came from club mosses of the Paleozoic. Today, these plants, the lycopods, are only a few inches high. They look like miniature cone-bearing evergreen trees, or conifers. They are easily missed when walking through a damp meadow. But during the Carboniferous they reached more than 100 feet (30 m). Interestingly, the lycopod trees had little wood and lots of bark.

Today's club moss still grows in damp settings. ↰

The primary coal-making plants of Gondwana were the tree ferns called *Glossopteris*. They stood about 12 feet (3.6 m) tall. *Glossopteris* fossils gave evidence to naturalists in the nineteenth century who first suggested that the continents were once joined together in a supercontinent. These fossils are found in bands that connect South America and Africa. They became extinct during the Triassic Period.

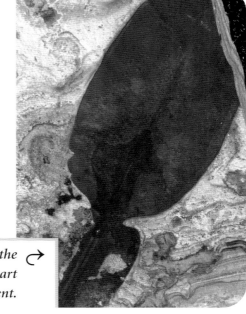

Glossopteris fossils are found throughout the southern continents that once were part of the Gondwana supercontinent. ↱

A museum painting of a coal-making swamp from the Pennsylvanian Epoch ↻

Coal beds can be amazing places to find fossils. This is because the coal usually alternates with layers of shale. The mud and sand that formed shale easily preserved the bodies of plants and animals. Dinosaurs, birds, or squirrels did not likely live among the trees of the coal swamps. There were many other animals, however. There were fish in the water, salamanders on the shore, dragonflies and other large insects flitting among the leaves. Worms, spiders, millipedes, and cockroaches—some amazingly large—clung to the soil. Sometimes large chunks of upright fossilized trees are found in coal.

The layers of coal and shale show that shallow seas moved in and out during the coal-making periods. A shale layer was usually formed from the soil in which the next coal-making trees grew when the seas had retreated. Such layers of coal are usually mined from the surface by strip mining.

A dark layer of coal often lies between shale and other sedimentary rocks. Such layers indicate changes in climate ↻

More Days in a Year

The year is the period Earth takes to revolve once around the sun. Many scientists now think that the year had more days during the Paleozoic than it has now. They think the year got progressively shorter. The number of days dropped from 408 days in a year to perhaps only 380. Today, it has only 365 1/4 days.

It wasn't that Earth took longer to go around the sun. Instead, the planet turned on its axis faster. The temperature difference between night and day would have been smaller than it is today. Thus, in the warm, moist surroundings of Laurentia, the coal forests grew more quickly and to greater size than before or since.

Seas may have moved in and out one hundred times over a hundred million years of the late Paleozoic. These million-year seas lasted a much shorter time than previous marine sea flooding had. The shorter time may have been due to changes in sea level that were happening around the globe. The up-down spasms of the Laurentian rock core itself were more likely the cause, however. The rock was reacting to the stresses of collisions at the boundaries of the North American plate.

During the middle of the Permian Period, Earth suddenly went through a much more arid, or dry, period. Swamps had supported the jungle-like growth that produced coal. These swamps then dried up. The primary coal-building period was over. Instead, the important plants of the future would be the seed plants. These plants had the reproductive means to survive periods of dryness. Conifers would soon take over much of the planet's plant-growing surface.

↰ *Conifers bear their seeds on cones, such as on this pine.*

Petroleum

Coal was not the only fossil fuel produced during the later Paleozoic. Petroleum, or oil, is also formed from the remains of living things. Coal was formed from giant trees. Petroleum, however, was formed from the tiniest creatures that lived in the warm shallow seas, such as **plankton** and algae. When plankton and algae died, they settled to the claylike bottom of the sea in quiet, undisturbed areas. Together, the clay and remains of the living things made a thick, black ooze.

Sometimes the ooze formed in areas where there was not much oxygen in the water. Dead plants and animals could not rot without oxygen. Such places might be found at the bottom of lakes or in caves on the bottom of the sea. And then, like coal, the ooze was covered over with sediment. It gradually turned to a kind of shale called black organic shale.

Over millions of years, the shale was buried deep enough to become warm. It became denser from the weight of the material above it. The shale was gradually transformed into petroleum. This is a thick, black substance made up mostly of **hydrocarbons**, which are different combinations of the chemical elements carbon and hydrogen. The hydrocarbons then moved into a rock containing many tiny spaces, such as limestone or sandstone. The fuel called natural gas usually forms in pockets above petroleum.

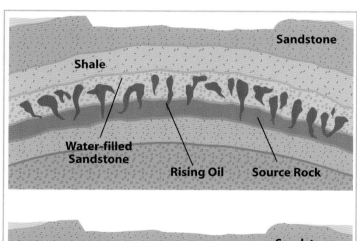

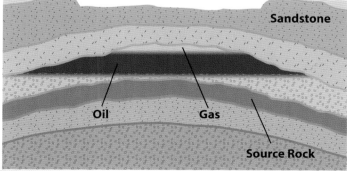

Petroleum forms within plant-bearing shale (top). It then moves into rock that has pores, where it is stored (bottom).

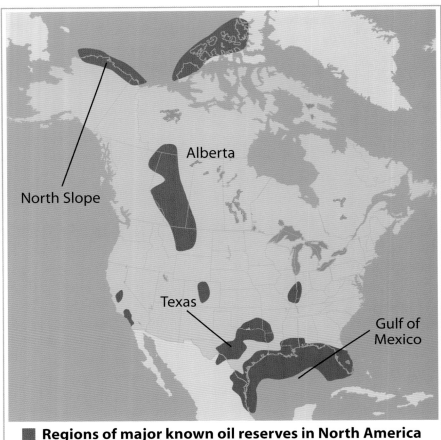

Petroleum from Alaska's North Slope goes through an above-ground pipeline to an ice-free port. There it is loaded on tankers for shipment to refineries. As the map shows, the North Slope is one of several areas of known oil reserves in North America.

North Slope

Alberta

Texas

Gulf of Mexico

■ **Regions of major known oil reserves in North America**

The petroleum-producing area of western Texas is called the Permian Basin. During the Permian Period, this area sank and formed a bowl-like basin. The Permian sea was mostly trapped in this basin and gradually evaporated. Petroleum pockets formed within the folds and faults of the reef-formed limestone rock. The first commercially useful oil wells were found in the Permian Basin in the early 1920s. Major oil fields also exist offshore around the rim of the Gulf of Mexico.

Canada's primary oil fields are located in the province of Alberta in an area called the Alberta Basin. These oil fields were laid down primarily in rocks of the Devonian Period.

Fossils of the Glass Mountains

The Glass Mountains are located in southwest Texas in an area known as the Permian Basin. They consist of sedimentary rock, such as limestone, shale, and sandstone. Their thick sedimentary layers date almost entirely from the Permian Period.

The area was underwater during the Permian. It now contains layers of various salts left from the evaporated inland sea. The area is also now a major producer of petroleum.

The Glass Mountains got their name from the glassy appearance of the many Permian fossils found there. The fossils are those of marine plants and animals that once lived in the ancient warm and shallow inland sea. Many of the fossils serve as excellent index fossils for other Permian rock layers in North America.

A fossil amphibian ↩

↩   A glassy-looking cephalopod fossil

Chapter 5

The Mystery of the Mass Extinction

When the geologic time scale was being developed, the end of the Paleozoic Era was set at the time when almost all living things suddenly disappeared. Known today as the Permian Extinction, its actual cause is still debated.

The Permian Extinction is also called the Permian-Triassic Extinction, or P-T Extinction. This indicates that it formed the boundary between the Permian Period of the Paleozoic and the Triassic Period of the Mesozoic. Recently, geologists pinpointed the dividing line between the Permian and the Triassic as exactly 248 million years ago.

The Permian Period started with many forms of life on land and in the sea. When the Permian ended, most were gone, including this Dimetrodon reptile.

At least 80 percent and possibly as many as 95 percent of all plant and animal species disappeared. Tropical communities were the hardest hit, especially reef-living animals. Some of the victims included all trilobites, two major types of corals and bryozoans, most ammonoids, and many early experiments in the ancestors of mammals.

The Permian Extinction was the largest extinction in biological history. It ended 57 percent of plant and animal families and 83 percent of smaller groups called **genera**. However, there were survivors. Those animals that could move freely among different kinds of environments generally survived to evolve further.

There is no single cause for the Permian Extinction. Several death-dealing events happened at approximately the same time. They happened within a period of a million years. The combination made each event worse than it would have been alone.

Basalt floods turned into the rock of huge areas along Washington's Columbia River. Note the steplike cliffs in the middle of the picture.

Great Lava Flows

A rock area in Siberia is called the Siberian **Traps**. It is a huge region of **igneous rock** that developed as the result of the largest known volcanic eruption in the history of the earth. (Such regions are called traps from the Swedish word *trapp*, meaning "staircase," from the steplike structure of the lava rock.)

Volcanic lava can flow over a large area and for a long time. Such episodes are called **basalt floods**. The lava that pours out hardens as the rock called **basalt**. These incredibly large and long-lasting eruptions are caused by a giant **heat plume** within the mantle of the planet. A huge layer of molten **magma** collects at the top of the plume. It must go somewhere, so it oozes out of any weak spots or holes in the planet's crust over vast areas. It then hardens as rock.

The area in Siberia, east of the Ural Mountains, in which the Siberian Traps erupted, was extremely large. It was so vast that if the lava were distributed across the entire planet, it would make a layer perhaps 13 feet (4 m) thick. About 248 million years ago, lava poured out of the ground for less than a million years. This is very brief for a basalt flood.

No one knows what causes a heat plume (also called a mantle plume) to rise from the hot core of the planet up through the mantle.

A heat plume that rises under a continent may cause the development of a chain of volcanic mountains to form. Often, the heat melts the underpart of the lithosphere. A huge flat area of basalt magma forms. This magma oozes out onto the crust.

The question is: Could the Siberian Traps have caused a massive extinction on Pangea? Geologists point to the largest recorded volcanic eruption. It took place at Laki, Iceland, for eight months starting in 1783. A "mere" 2.9 cubic miles (14.7 cubic km) of lava poured out over 218 square miles (565 sq km) of land. The poisonous gases given off were enough to kill most of the crops. By blocking the sun, they lowered the planet's temperature about 1.8°F (1°C).

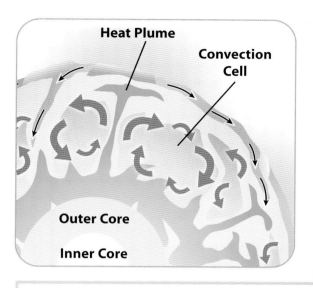

A heat plume is a shaft of heat that rises through the mantle toward the lithosphere, where rock may melt.

The Heat Plume at Yellowstone

Basalt floods are not frequent occurrences. The last known one started about 17 million years ago when one formed a vast region through which the Columbia River cuts in Washington and Oregon. The same heat plume is still active. As the North American tectonic plate moved, the heat plume built volcanic land in Idaho. Today, it is still heating the lithosphere under Yellowstone National Park. There it shows itself as the geysers and heated pools of the world's first national park. Minerva Spring, a hot spring shown here, deposits a mineral called travertine, which makes spectacular terraces.

Scientists suggest that during the flow of the Siberian Traps, sulfur, carbon dust, ash, and poisonous gases were caught up in the global winds. They blocked sunlight, preventing plants from carrying on photosynthesis. This also quickly dropped the planet's temperature. As a result, huge ice caps formed. The formation of the ice caps would require vast quantities of water from the oceans. This would cause sea level to drop abruptly. This was all in addition to the poisonous gases and acid rain that normally accompany a volcanic eruption.

Sulfur, a yellow chemical element, can collect around a steam vent on a volcano. When blown by wind, sulfur is one of the poisons that might have added to the Permian Extinction.

Death from Outer Space

Scientists studying the Permian Extinction looked at the rapid extinction of the dinosaurs at the end of the Mesozoic Era. This event is called the **Cretaceous-Tertiary Extinction**, also known as the K-T Extinction. In 1980, Nobel Prize-winner Luis Alvarez and his son Walter discovered a thin layer of sediments that was deeply buried around the whole planet. The layer contained a great deal of the rare element iridium. The layer would have formed in geologic time just when the dinosaurs died off.

Father and son knew that iridium is rarely found on Earth except in **meteorites**. These are rocky bits that enter the planet's atmosphere and survive to reach the ground. They calculated that a meteorite might have struck Earth 65 million years ago. They estimated that such a rock from solar orbit must have been about 6 miles (10 km) across. It was traveling at a speed that would have made a crater more than 62 miles (100 km) in diameter. At first, geologists thought that the meteorite struck the western United States. Then other studies showed it probably struck Yucatan in Mexico. An estimated 55 percent of all species died out.

Meteor Crater in Arizona is an impact crater formed when a meteorite struck Earth about 50,000 years ago. It was the first landform to be identified as an impact crater.

Did something similar happen earlier, at the Permian-Triassic boundary? Few scientists jumped on the meteorite bandwagon right away. However, some 21st-century discoveries in Antarctica have been made that are causing scientists to reconsider. Round nuggets of various metals and meteor fragments discovered in layers of rock were formed at the end of the Permian. Similar minerals have been found in China. Some scientists think that a large-scale event occurred. It was probably an impact with an extraterrestrial body, or perhaps the debris-carrying tail of a **comet**.

A petroleum geologist thinks he has found evidence near Australia of a circular structure about 125 miles (200 km) in diameter. This might possibly be a crater formed by the impact of a meteorite. Other geologists think that the heat caused by an impact in the Permian would have been so great that the crust would melt. There would now be no sign of an impact crater to be found.

An artist's idea of the impact of a meteorite from outer space. Life near the impact would be instantly wiped out by the high temperatures and pressures.

Canada's Impact Crater

Visible from space, an impact crater lies in the Canadian Shield of the Canadian province of Quebec. Called the Manicougan Crater, it is about 60 miles (97 km) across. Some scientists thought that it might have played a role in either the Permian Extinction or the one at the end of the Mesozoic Era that killed off the dinosaurs. However, it probably occurred between the two extinctions, about 214 million years ago.

The sides of the deep crater collapsed and filled in the center. The remaining circle filled with water and became a ring-shaped lake.

Pangea's Climate

The supercontinent Pangea was huge. Its size may have played a role in the Permian Extinction. With such a huge landmass, major climate systems would have been more severe than anything humans have ever known.

The extinction may actually have been a double event. There were two smaller episodes of great change in the environment. These may have built up into one huge extinction. One reason paleontologists think that two episodes may have happened is that many species of certain foraminiferans disappeared before the Permian Extinction. These creatures were no bigger than a grain of wheat. Their extinction may have happened 5 million years before the main extinction began.

Climate changes were already underway. Carboniferous swamps gave way to huge deserts in the Permian. This happened as the level of the sea dropped drastically. There was not enough sea for the animals to survive in. However, sea level changes generally have happened at a much slower rate

Certain species of the single-celled shelled creatures called ↱ *forams disappeared in what might have been a minor extinction before the big Permian Extinction.*

than would have caused the P-T Extinction. It still took probably 8 million years. That's far different, however, from the 40 to 50 million years of other such changes.

Plant species on land changed during the late Paleozoic as the environment changed. There was a major **glaciation** on Gondwana. This created a cool, wet climate in Laurentia. The continent was moving northward toward the equator during the early Permian. It began to warm up and the climate turned drier and hotter. This forced plants to change character. Conifers and seed plants, for example, replaced tree ferns.

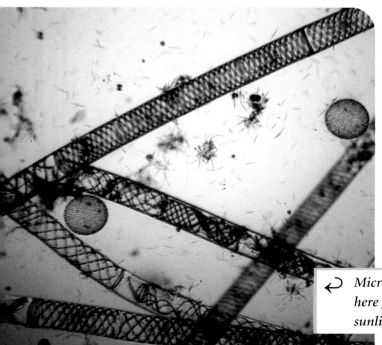

Enter the Siberian Traps. The materials that were spewed out in the lava would have changed the atmosphere. They would have prevented the normal amount of sunlight from reaching the plants, both on land and in the sea. Without the plants that make up an important part of plankton, marine animals would starve.

↰ *Microscopic marine plants, such as these shown here greatly magnified, died off from lack of sunlight at the end of the Permian.*

The central part of Pangea became a great desert. Moisture-loving ferns were replaced by plants that could live in harsh conditions.

There is also evidence that the water in the single huge ocean called Panthalassa suffered from lack of oxygen at the same time. The planet's temperature increased suddenly by at least 11°F (6°C). One effect of such an increase is a decrease in the amount of oxygen in the ocean water. This lack of oxygen alone might have killed off many marine creatures.

In addition, there is a phenomenon in some seafloors of the world called gas hydrates. These are icelike structures formed by a mixture of water and **methane** (which is a hydrocarbon natural gas). They are known to form in pores or openings in sediment layers. This happens when conditions— especially cold temperatures and high pressures—are right.

Gas hydrates are known occasionally to break open. They then release the methane gas within. Some scientists have suggested that gas hydrates could have been released on a massive scale. Methane gas is poisonous. Such a release would have poisoned both the water and the atmosphere. Few creatures could have survived.

Scientists don't yet know for sure just what caused the Permian Extinction, when Earth's life almost died. They may never know for sure— 248 million years in the past is a long time ago. But it may have happened because of a combination of two or three of the possibilities mentioned.

It may have been all of them together. Or it may have been something that has not even been suggested yet.

Life, having started on the planet, is very determined. It hangs on for all its worth. A mere 5 percent of the species that had developed were left at the end of the Paleozoic. This was enough for evolution of plants and animals to resume at full steam during the Mesozoic Era.

Curt Teichert wrote in 1990, "The way in which many Paleozoic life forms disappeared towards the end of the Permian Period brings to mind Joseph Haydn's *Farewell Symphony* where, during the last movement, one musician after the other takes his instrument and leaves the stage until, at the end, none is left." Fortunately for Earth's life, the Permian Extinction did not end with an empty stage.

During the next geological era, the Mesozoic, the North American "stage" would be completed. The life that almost died would evolve into the fascinating dinosaurs. However, they, too, would later face extinction.

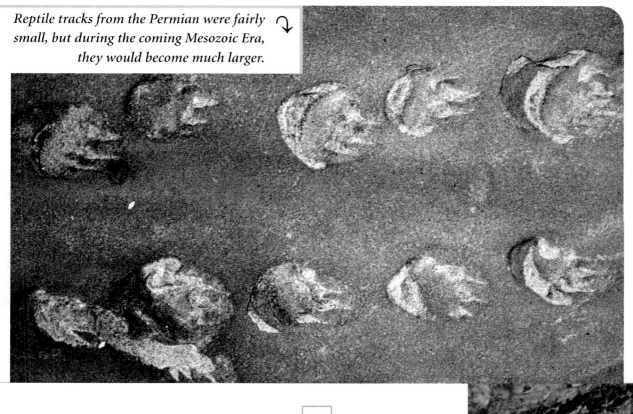

Reptile tracks from the Permian were fairly small, but during the coming Mesozoic Era, they would become much larger.

GEOLOGIC TIME SCALE

PRECAMBRIAN TIME • 4.5 billion to 543 million years ago

Time Period	Tectonic Events	Biological Events
Hadean Eon *4.5–3.96 billion years ago* Named for Hades, or Hell	No Earth rocks from this time found	None
Archean Eon *3.96–2.5 billion years ago* Name means "Ancient"	Oldest known rocks First permanent crust First stable continents	Seawater formed First bacteria Atmosphere formed
Proterozoic Eon *2.5 billion–543 million*	North American craton formed First iron–bearing sediments First large glaciation Formation and breakup of Rodinia supercontinent Gondwana, southern supercontinent, formed	Free oxygen in atmosphere First nucleated cells, allowing sexual reproduction First multicellular animals First animals with exoskeletons First fungi

PHANEROZOIC TIME • 543 million years ago to present

PALEOZOIC ERA • 543 to 248 million years ago

Time Period	Tectonic Events	Biological Events
Cambrian Period *543–248 million years ago* Named for old name of Wales	Laurentia separated from Siberia	Cambrian Explosion: Major diversification of marine invertebrates
Ordovician Period *490–443 million years ago* Named for a Celtic tribe in Wales	First Iapetus Ocean Taconic orogeny in northeastern Laurentia	First true vertebrates: jawless fish First land plants Mass extinction
Silurian Period *443–417 million years ago* Named for a Celtic tribe in Wales	Caledonian orogeny Shallow seas on Laurentia	First vascular plants First insects First jawed fish
Devonian Period *417–354 million years ago* Named for Devon, England	Major reef building	First forests First seed–baring plants First four–footed animals First amphibians
CARBONIFEROUS PERIOD 354 to 290 million years ago — **Mississippian Epoch** *354–323 million years ago* Named for Mississippi River Valley	Antler orogeny	Ferns abundant First land vertebrates
Pennsylvanian Epoch *323–290 million years ago* Named for coal formations in Pennsylvania	Appalachian orogeny began Antler orogeny	Ferns abundant Major coal–forming forests First reptiles
Permian *290–248 million years ago* Named for Russian province of Perm	Pangea formed	First warm–blooded reptiles Greatest mass extinction

	Time Period	Tectonic Events	Biological Events	
MESOZOIC ERA 248 to 65 million years ago	**Triassic Period** *248–206 million years ago* Named for three layers in certain European rocks	Pangea completed Major part of Pangea was arid	First flying vertebrates First dinosaurs First mammals Cephalopods abundant	
	Jurassic Period *206–144 million hears ago* Named for the Jura Mountains	Atlantic began to open Pangea separated into Gondwana and Laurasia	First birds Cycads abundant	
	Cretaceous Period *144–65 million years ago* Named after Latin word for "chalk"	Major volcanism Sevier orogeny Laurentia separated from Eurasia Sierra Nevada batholith	First flowering plants First social insects Mass extinction of dinosaurs	

		Time Period	Tectonic Events	Biological Events	
PHANEROZOIC TIME • 543 million years ago to present / **CENOZOIC ERA • 65 million years ago to present**	**TERTIARY PERIOD • 65 to 1.8 million years ago**	**Paleocene Epoch** *65 to 54.8 million years ago*	Laramide orogeny Western Laurentia uplifted	Mammals and birds diversified First horse ancestors	
		Eocene Epoch *54.8 to 33.7 million years ago*	Rockies uplifted Global cooling began	First mammals (whales) in sea First primates First cats and dogs	
		Oligocene Epoch *33.7 to 23.8 million years ago*	North Atlantic opened Ice cap formed in Anatarctica	First apes Grasslands widespread	
		Miocene Epoch *23.8 to 5.3 million years ago*	Columbia flood basalts	First human ancestors First mastodons	
		Pliocene Epoch *5.3 to 1.8 million years ago*	Northern Hemisphere glaciation began Cascade Volcanoes	Large mammals abundant	
	QUATERNARY PERIOD *1.8 million to today*	**Pleistocene Epoch** *1.8 million years ago to today*	Great glaciation of Northern Hemisphere	First modern humans Extinction of large mammals Humans entered North America	
		Holocene *10,000 years ago to today*	Rifting continued in East Africa Human–caused global warming	Human-caused extinctions	

accretion the addition of terrane to a tectonic plate. This increase typically occurs through the process of subduction.

algae (singular is **alga**) simple, usually one-celled marine plants, such as seaweed or pond scum, with natural green color often hidden by brown or red tint; contain chlorophyll and lack roots, stems, and leaves.

ammonoid marine animal with a flat, coiled, chambered shell. These are cephalopod mollusks that date from the Devonian to the Cretaceous periods. Some had long tentacles or arms.

amphibian a cold-blooded vertebrate (animal with a backbone) that is able to live both on land and in water. Amphibians include frogs and salamanders.

anthracite hard coal which is more than 95% carbon but low in volatile (rapidly evaporating) hydrocarbons; burns with little or no flame.

arthropod any of a group of animals that has a jointed body and limbs and a segmented outer shell called an exoskeleton. Arthropods include spiders and insects.

asthenosphere the part of Earth's mantle that lies beneath the lithosphere. This zone of soft, easily deformed rock is believed to be less rigid, hotter, and more fluid than the rock above or below.

Baltica one of six major continents that formed during the Paleozoic Era. It was composed of Scandinavia, Poland, Russia west of the Ural Mountains, and northern Germany.

basalt dark, dense, volcanic, igneous rock. Basalt makes up most of the ocean floor.

basalt flood large, long-lasting volcanic eruption that occurs over a vast area. The lava or molten rock that pours out is primarily basalt.

basin a low area, or depression, in the earth's surface that collects sediment. In the sea, this depression is cut off from ocean currents.

bedding layering of sedimentary rocks

bituminous a soft coal that contains bitumen and other volatile (rapidly evaporating) hydrocarbons and tarlike matter; burns with a smoky, yellow flame.

bryozoan marine or freshwater animal that lives in groups of its own kind, or colonies. Also called moss animals, these creatures are stationary and their shells can make up reefs.

cephalopod mollusk having tentacles attached to its head; includes the squid, octopus, and nautilus. *Cephalopod* literally means "head foot."

coal sedimentary rock derived from partially decomposed, carbonized plant matter. This black or dark brown mineral substance is used as fuel.

comet a large ball made of ice and dust that circles the sun in the solar system in a predicable orbit

conifer a type of tree or shrub that is generally evergreen, has needle-like leaves, and bears its seeds on cones, such as pines

Cordillera the region of the western part of North America that includes all the mountain ranges parallel to the Pacific Coast, from Mexico through Alaska

Cretaceous-Tertiary Extinction event that occurred 65 million years ago during which the dinosaurs became extinct or died off quickly. About 85% of all species were wiped out. Also called the K-T Extinction.

crinoid sea animal that has a cup-shaped body with branched, radiating arms. Today's crinoids include sea lilies and feather stars.

crust outermost, rocky layer of Earth. This low-density layer is about 22 miles (35 km) thick under continents and 6 miles (10 km) thick under oceans.

cycad a palmlike tropical plant that evolved during the Paleozoic. Only a few species remain today.

deformation a change in shape, dimension, or volume of rocks because of folding, faulting, and other processes that result from stress or strain

epoch a division of geologic time next shorter than a period. In the Paleozoic Era, the Carboniferous Period is divided into two epochs.

evolution development of a species or other group of organisms; the theory that all existing organisms are related and developed from earlier forms of organisms

fault a fracture, or break, in rock along which each side moves relative to each other. Sudden faults are experienced as earthquakes.

fold noticeable curve in the layering of sedimentary or metamorphic rock; large-scale folds make mountains.

fold thrust a fold in sedimentary rock that has been pushed horizontally over other land

foraminiferan (or **foram**) marine protozoan that typically has a linear, spiral, or concentric shell; they made up a large part of the plankton that filled the seas during the Cambrian and Devonian periods.

fossil evidence or trace of animal or plant life of a past geological age. These typically mineralized remains have been preserved in rocks of the earth's crust. Traces include bones and footprints of extinct land animals, such as dinosaurs.

fossil fuel coal, petroleum, or natural gas, because each was the result of long term changes in ancient plants and animals

genera (plural of **genus**) major subdivisions in a biological family or subfamily in the classification of organisms. Genera usually are made up of more than one species.

geologic time scale a calendar that establishes distinct time periods in the history of the earth. The time is shown in millions of years. The geologic time scale used in this book is on pages 72 and 73.

glaciation the process of becoming covered by ice or glaciers. It refers to a period of geological time when global cooling occurred and ice sheets covered large areas of the earth.

glacier a mass of very dense ice on land that moves slowly, either by coming down from high mountains or spreading out across land from a central point where ice has accumulated

gneiss a coarse-grained, metamorphic rock, made up of bands that differ in color and composition

Gondwana supercontinent in the Southern Hemisphere that began to separate from Pangea toward the end of the Paleozoic Era. It contained present-day South America, Africa, southern Europe, the peninsula of India, Australia, and Antarctica.

granite coarse-grained, intrusive rock. Granite is composed of sodium and potassium feldspar primarily, but it is also rich in quartz. Light in color, it is a common rock in North America.

groundwater water that moves beneath the surface of the ground; the source of well water and springs

heat plume column of hot material in the earth's mantle that rises toward the lithosphere; also called mantle plume

hydrocarbon a chemical compound that contains both hydrogen and carbon

igneous rock rock formed directly from magma when it has cooled and solidified. *Igneous* means "fiery."

index fossil an animal or plant fossil that is representative of a certain time period. Index fossils are well-defined and easily identifiable, plentiful, and spread widely throughout an area during a relatively short range of time.

island arc a curved or arc-shaped chain of volcanic islands lying near a continent that form as a result of a subduction zone, such as the Aleutian chain in Alaska

larvae newly hatched insects that are wormlike and lacks wings, such as caterpillars. Animals such as brachiopods also develop from larvae, which are young without shells that can swim about freely.

Laurentia a large continent formed during the Paleozoic Era from which the modern continent of North America developed. It was composed mostly of North America and Greenland.

lava fluid, molten rock, or magma, that emerges from a volcano or volcanic vent to the earth's surface. When lava is cooled and solidified, it forms an igneous rock such as basalt.

lignite a soft coal, usually dark brown, with a woodlike texture. In carbon content and density it is between peat and bituminous coal.

limestone a type of sedimentary rock, made up of more than 50% of calcium carbonate ($CaCO_3$), primarily as the mineral calcite, which may be mixed with sediments or mud

lithosphere the hard outer layer of Earth containing the outer part of Earth's mantle and its crust. It consists of tectonic plates that float on the asthenosphere.

lycopod a plant that bears cones at the branch tips; also called club moss

magma molten rock that exists beneath Earth's crust. Molten rock that flows to the surface is called lava.

mammal a warm-blooded vertebrate animal that feeds its young on its mother's milk; includes both pouched and nonpouched animals

mantle thick part of Earth's interior that lies between the crust and the outer core. Along with the crust, the upper mantle forms the plates of plate tectonics.

marine relating or pertaining to the sea

marsupial a primitive mammal that gives birth to very undeveloped young and carries them in a pouch as they continue to develop; most marsupials live in Australia

mass extinction event during the earth's history when many species of living things became extinct, or were killed off, due to drastic changes in sea levels.

meteorite mass of matter that has reached Earth from outer space

methane colorless, odorless, flammable gas (CH_4). A hydrocarbon like natural gas, it is found in marsh gas.

mollusk a marine invertebrate (animal without a backbone), such as shellfish

molten liquefied by heat

nautilus tropical marine mollusk that lives in a spiral shell. The shell is divided into chambers filled with air.

orogeny process by which mountains are built. This process involves folding, faulting, and uplifting of the earth's crust.

paleontology the study of forms of life that existed in past geological periods through study of their fossils

Pangea (also written **Pangaea**) the supercontinent made up of most landmasses and covering about 25 percent of Earth's surface. Formed by the end of the Paleozoic Era, it lasted more than 100 million years.

Panthalassa Ocean the single, planet-wide ocean that surrounded the supercontinent Pangea during the Paleozoic Era

peat partly decayed plant matter deposited in a wet environment, such as a marsh or swamp. Peat is used as fuel and contains more than 50% carbon.

Permian Extinction time at the end of the Paleozoic Era when almost all living things became extinct, or died out. Scientists estimate that almost 95% of all animal and plant species were wiped out.

photosynthesis process by which plants form their own food from carbon dioxide and water through the action of sunlight on a green chemical called chlorophyll. A by-product or waste product of this process is oxygen

plankton organisms, such as microscopic algae and protozoa, that passively float or drift within a body of water and feed many animals

plateau a large area of uplifted rock that appears to be fairly flat on top

province a generally large area of crust in which the rock has undergone about the same geologic history

quartzite a metamorphic rock composed of the mineral quartz and deriving from quartz sandstone but without the grains cemented together

reef large mound or ridge within a body of water, made from the skeletons of organisms such as corals and sponges cemeneted together

reptile an air-breathing vertebrate (animal with a backbone) that lives on land, including snakes, turtles, lizards, crocodiles, as well as other extinct creatures.

sandstone common sedimentary rock made up of sand, including quartz, that is cemented together by silica, clay, calcium carbonate, or iron oxide

schist a type of metamorphic rock that forms in thin layers. It is derived from fine-grained sedimentary rock such as shale.

sediment loose, uncemented pieces of rock or minerals carried and deposited by water, air, or ice. Sediment may include eroded sand, dirt particles, debris from living things, and solid materials that form as a result of chemical processes.

sedimentary rock rock composed of sediment. Examples include sandstone and limestone. Sedimentary rock typically forms beds, or layers.

shale finely layered, laminated sedimentary rock derived from mud; the non-laminated variety is known as mudstone. It is formed by the consolidation of clay, mud, or silt.

Siberia one of six major continents during the Paleozoic Era. It became much of Russia east of the Ural Mountains.

sphenopsid ancestor of today's horsetails. Some grew as trees; most became extinct after the Paleozoic.

spores the fertilized bodies of a non-flowering plant or fungus. The organism sheds spores to reproduce itself, similar to the way seed or pollen is shed.

spreading ridge undersea area where tectonic plates are pushed apart on the mantle. The ridge forms a line that twists and turns around the ocean floor.

subduction the process by which oceanic crust moves down into the asthenosphere beneath a continental plate; occurs at trenches, called subduction zones

supercontinent any of several giant landmasses formed during past geologic times and made up of several present-day continents

synapsid a now-extinct reptile that had an opening in its skull to which muscles were attached; though to be an ancestor of mammals

tectonic plate large section of Earth's lithosphere that floats on the asthenosphere and moves independently, sometimes rubbing against other plates

terrane a fragment of crust that is bounded on all sides by faults and which has a geologic history that differs from neighboring blocks. It may be made from island arcs or a piece of a tectonic plate.

trace fossil an impression or outline of any plant or animal preserved in rock. It gives partial evidence of a larger form of life. A fossilized footprint is an example of a trace fossil.

trap dark colored, fine-grained igneous rock, such as basalt. Traps have a steplike appearance. The term comes from the Swedish word *trapp* for "staircase.". The Siberian Traps formed as a result of the largest known volcanic eruption in Earth's history.

uplift process in which a portion of the earth's crust is raised as a result of heat within the mantle. The crust can also be raised in response to tectonic forces, or large scale movements deep within the surface.

vascular refers to plants that have water in their tissues so that they can stand erect. The first vascular plants were found in Silurian rocks.

weathering erosion of rock by the elements of weather, such as wind and rain, which gradually break it up into sediment particles

FURTHER INFORMATION

ONLINE WEB SITES

Museum of Paleontology
University of California at Berkeley
1101 Valley Life Sciences Building
Berkeley, CA 94720
www.ucmp.berkeley.edu/exhibit/exhibits.html
takes you through major exhibits in geology,
evolution, and the classification of living things
Also produced by UCMP is:
www.paleoportal.org
provides a link to many sites for anyone
interested in paleontology

United States Geological Survey
USGS National Center
12201 Sunrise Valley Drive
Reston, VA 20192
www.usgs.gov/education
The Learning Web introduces numerous topics and
projects related to earth science
Find out what's happening at Mount St. Helens
volcano: http://volcanoes.usgs.gov
or where the earthquakes are:
http://earthquake.usgs.gov

The British Broadcasting Corporation has major coverage of prehistoric life:
http://www.bbc.co.uk

MUSEUMS

Be sure to look for museum web sites. Also, be sure to check university and public
museums in your area; they often have good geology exhibits.

UNITED STATES
American Museum of Natural History
Central Park West at 79th St.
New York, NY 10024
www.amnh.org

Colorado School of Mines Geology Museum
13th and Maple St.
Golden, CO 80401

The Field Museum
1400 S. Lake Shore Drive
Chicago, IL 60605
www.fieldmuseum.org
Look for the online exhibit about Sue, the best
preserved *Tyrannosaurus rex*

University of Michigan Museum of Paleontology
1109 Geddes Ave.,
Ann Arbor, MI 48109
www.paleontology.lsa.umich.edu

Smithsonian National Museum of Natural History
10th St. and Constitution Ave.
Washington, D.C. 20560
www.mnh.si.edu

CANADA
Geological Survey of Canada
Earth Sciences Sector
601 Booth St.
Ottawa, Ontario K1A 0E8, Canada
http://ess.nrcan.gc.ca

Canadian Museum of Nature
240 McLeod St.
Ottawa, Ontario K1P 6P4, Canada
www.nature.ca

Provincial Museum of Alberta
12845 102nd Ave.
Edmonton, Alberta T5N 0M6, Canada
www.prma.edmonton.ab.ca

Manitoba Museum of Man and Nature
190 Rupert Avenue
Winnipeg, Manitoba R3B 0N2, Canada
www.manitobamuseum.mb.ca

Pacific Museum of the Earth
6339 Stores Road
Vancouver, British Columbia V6T 1Z4, Canada
www.eos.ubc.ca

DVDs

Amazing Earth, Artisan Entertainment, 2001

Forces of Nature—Book and DVD, National Geographic, 2004

Living Rock: An Introduction to Earth's Geology, WEA Corp, 2002
Also includes 400 USGS "Fact Sheets" in Adobe Acrobat format, obtainable on computer sytems with a DVD-ROM Drive)

Physical Geography: Geologic Time, TMW/Media Group, 2004

Volcano: Nature's Inferno!, National Geographic, 1997

BOOKS

Anderson, Peter. *A Grand Canyon Journey: Tracing Time in Stone*. A First Book. Danbury, CT: Franklin Watts, 1997.

Ball, Jacqueline. *Earth's History*. Discovery Channel School Science series. Milwaukee, WI: Gareth Stevens Publishing, 2004.

Bonner, Hannah. *When Bugs Were Big : Prehistoric Life in a World Before Dinosaurs*. Washington, DC: National Geographic, 2004.

Castelfranchi, Yuri, and Nico Petrilli. *History of the Earth: Geology, Ecology, and Biology*. Hauppage, NY: Barrons, 2003.

Colson, Mary. *Earth Erupts*. Turbulent Earth series. Chicago: Raintree, 2005.

Colson, Mary. *Shaky Ground*. Turbulent Earth series. Chicago: Raintree, 2005.

Day, Trevor. *DK Guide to Savage Earth: An Earth Shattering Journey of Discovery*. New York: Dorling Kindersley, 2001.

Farndon, John. *How the Earth Works*. Pleasantville, NY: Reader's Digest, 1992.

Hooper, Meredith. *The Pebble in My Pocket: A History of Our Earth*. New York: Viking Books, 1996.

Lambert, David. *The Kingfisher Young People's Book of the Universe*. Boston: Kingfisher, 2001.

Maslin, Mark. *Earthquakes*. Restless Planet series. Chicago: Raintree, 2000.

Maynard, Christopher. *My Book of the Prehistoric World*. Boston: Kingfisher, 2001.

Oxlade, Chris. *The Earth and Beyond*. Chicago: Heinemann Library, 1999.

NOTE: All Internet addresses (URLs) listed in this book were valid at the time it went to press. However, due to the dynamic nature of the Internet, some addresses may have changed, or sites may have ceased to exist since publication. While the authors and publisher regret any inconvenience this may cause readers, no responsibility for any such changes can be accepted by either the authors or publisher.

INDEX